Days out in Winter

Vic Parker

Heinemann
LIBRARY

Little Nippers

www.heinemann.co.uk/library
Visit our website to find out more information about **Heinemann Library** books.

To order:
☎ Phone 44 (0) 1865 888066
▤ Send a fax to 44 (0) 1865 314091
▣ Visit the Heinemann Bookshop at www.heinemann.co.uk/library to browse our catalogue and order online.

First published in Great Britain by Heinemann Library, Halley Court, Jordan Hill, Oxford OX2 8EJ, part of Harcourt Education.
Heinemann is a registered trademark of Harcourt Education Ltd.

Editorial: Jilly Attwood and Claire Throp
Design: Jo Hinton-Malivoire and bigtop, Bicester, UK
Models made by: Jo Brooker
Picture Research: Rosie Garai, Sally Smith and Debra Weatherley
Production: Séverine Ribierre

Originated by Dot Gradations
Printed and bound in China by South China Printing Company

ISBN 0 431 17300 1 (hardback)
08 07 06 05 04
10 9 8 7 6 5 4 3 2 1

ISBN 0 431 17305 2 (paperback)
08 07 06 05
10 9 8 7 6 5 4 3 2

British Library Cataloguing in Publication Data
Parker, Vic
Days out in winter
508.2
A full catalogue record for this book is available from the British Library.

Acknowledgements
The publisher would like to thank the following for permission to reproduce photographs:
Ardea p. **7** (J. Marchington); Arena p. **16–17** (Colin Willoughby); Corbis p. **11** (Tom Stewart), p. **4**; Garden Picture Library p. **22** (Janet Sorrell); Gareth Boden p. **19**; Holt Studios p. **14**; Imagestate pp. **8**, **23**; Photofusion p. **15** (Libby Welch); Trevor Clifford pp. **5**, **9**, **10**, **12**, **13**; Trip p. **20–21** (D. Harding); Zefa p. **18** (K. Schafer).

Cover photograph reproduced with permission of Masterfile/Rommel.

The publishers would like to thank Annie Davy for her assistance in the preparation of this book.

Every effort has been made to contact copyright holders of any material reproduced in this book. Any omissions will be rectified in subsequent printings if notice is given to the publishers.

The paper used to print this book comes from sustainable resources.

Contents

It's wintertime!

Winter is the **coldest** time of the year.

4

hat

jumper

scarf

mittens

Wrap up **warm** before you go out.

Winter walk

On a frosty winter walk,
your shoulders **shiver**,
your teeth **chatter**
and your nose **glows**.

Feed the birds

Some wild animals go hungry in winter.

Get your skates on

These shoes look strange!

They are made especially for skating on ice!

Story time

It is **warm** and **cosy** in the library.

Are you sitting comfortably?

Christmas is coming

At Christmas time, do you go on a shopping trip to buy a tree?

If you are lucky, you might see Santa too!

Have you ever been to a pantomime?

Aquarium adventure

Would you like to see what is under the sea?

You can at an aquarium.

19

New Year celebration

Now a new year is about to begin. It's time to celebrate!

Snowy day

What turns the world white?
A shower of snow!

23

Index

The end

Notes for adults

The *Days out in...* series helps young children become familiar with the way their environment changes through the year. The books explore the natural world in each season and how this affects community life and social activities. Used together, the books will enable discussion about similarities and differences between the seasons, how the natural world follows a cyclical pattern, and how different people mark special dates in the year. The following Early Learning Goals are relevant to this series:

Knowledge and understanding of the world

Early learning goals for exploration and investigation
• look closely at similarities, differences, patterns and change.

Early learning goals for sense of time
• observe changes in the environment, for example through the seasons.

Early learning goals for cultures and beliefs
• begin to know about their own cultures and beliefs and those of other people.

This book introduces the reader to the season of winter. It will encourage young children to think about winter weather, wildlife and landscape; activities they can enjoy in winter; and what clothes it is appropriate to wear. The book will help children extend their vocabulary, as they will hear new words such as *frosty* and *pantomime*. You may like to introduce and explain other new words yourself, such as *ice rink* and *dragon dancers*.

Additional information about the seasons

Not all places in the world have four seasons. Climate is affected by two factors: 1) how near a place is to the Equator (hence how much heat it receives from the Sun), 2) how high a place is (mountains are cooler than nearby lowlands). This is why some parts of the world have just two seasons, such as the hot wet season and the hot dry season across much of India. Other parts of the world have just one season, such as the year-long heat of the Sahara desert or the year-long cold of the North Pole.

Follow-up activities

• Take a trip to an ice rink or indoor ski slope.
• Visit a library to find out more about Chinese New Year, or Christmas traditions and stories from other countries.
• Draw a picture of a snowman wearing some winter clothes and decorate it with buttons, ribbon, etc.